TRACKING NOKOMIS

One Maine Bird's Journey to Haiti and Back

TAMMY CLOUTIER

illustrations by MICHAEL BOARDMAN

Tracking Nokomis
One Maine Bird's Journey to Haiti and Back

by TAMMY CLOUTIER
with illustrations by MICHAEL BOARDMAN

Cover and book design by
RENDER design + publications
renderpublications.com

ISBN: 979-8-9873471-1-9

Published by Tammy Cloutier
canidsrule@gmail.com

DEDICATION

Thank you to Danielle D'Auria (waterbird specialist extraordinaire)
for letting me play citizen scientist and introducing me to GBHs.
Your time, patience, and graciousness from when this idea first took
flight to seeing Nokomis finally land on paper are greatly appreciated!

And thank you to the wildlife who continue to teach and show us
humans just how amazing you and this planet we share are.
The world would be empty without you.

Meet Nokomis

Meet Nokomis.
(pronounced *noh-KOH-miss*)
Nokomis is a Native American word that means "grandmother" or "the great mother."

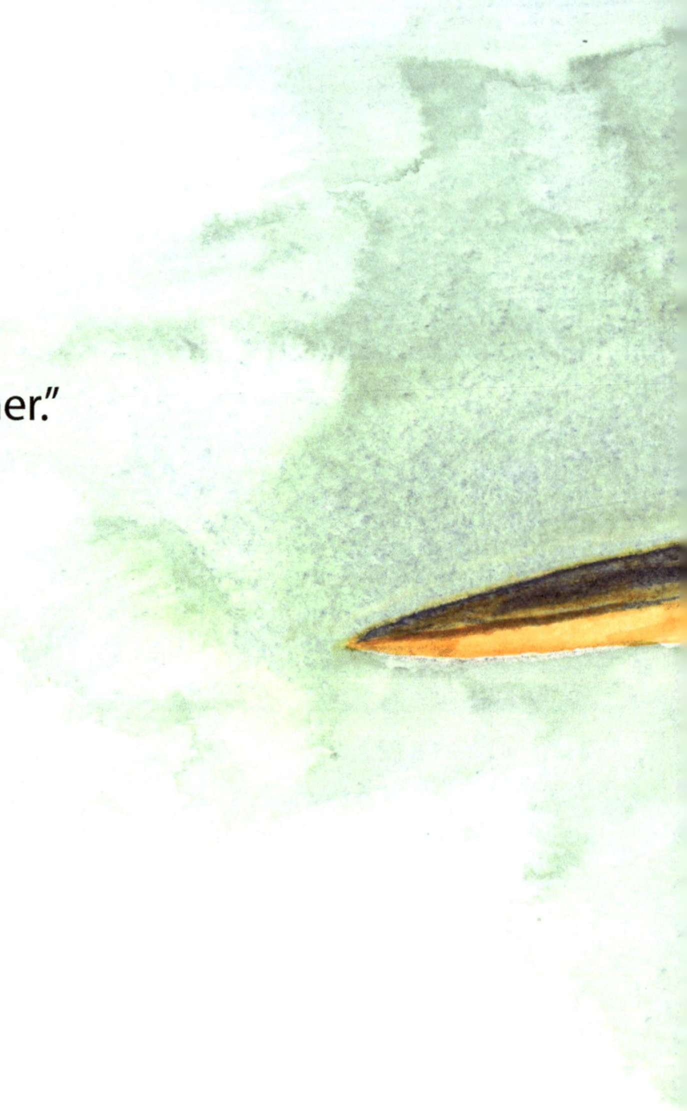

But this Nokomis is a Great Blue Heron. Nokomis got her name because she was found by students from Nokomis Regional High School in Newport, Maine.

Wildlife biologists wanted to learn more about great blue herons
and Nokomis was one of many great blue herons who were "tagged."
"Tagged" means that a small tracking device was placed on Nokomis'
back. This device collected information about where Nokomis
traveled, and the students and biologists could follow along.

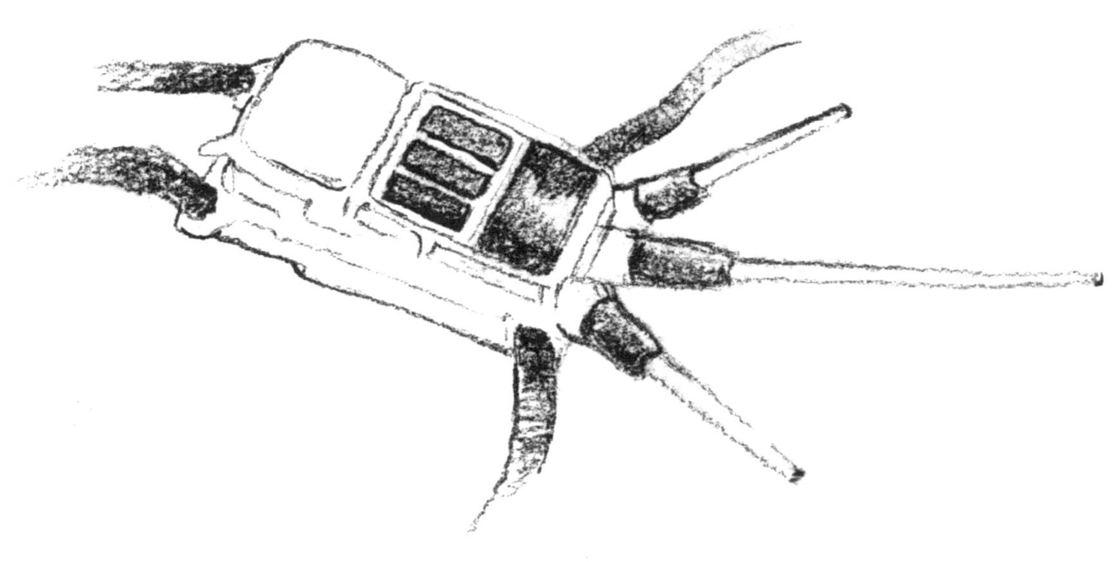

Nokomis spent the spring and summer in Maine. When autumn arrived, it was time for her to migrate.

Migration means that Nokomis had to leave Maine so she could spend the winter in a warmer place with more food.

Nokomis knew she needed to eat a lot to have energy to make the long trip. She stood as still as a statue in a pond watching for any movement in the water. Then a fish swam by. She grabbed it with her sharp bill and swallowed it whole! After eating lots of fish for several days, she was ready.

It was early evening when Nokomis pushed off the
ground, tucked her long neck into the shape of an "S,"
and flapped her giant wings – leaving Maine behind.

Nokomis flew for most of the night. By dawn, she was tired and hungry and noticed a marsh with other great blue herons. As she landed to join them, two frogs hopped by her feet. She quickly caught and swallowed them. Then she settled down to rest, keeping one eye open to make sure she was safe in this new place. Every now and then she would see movement in the water and catch another fish or frog.

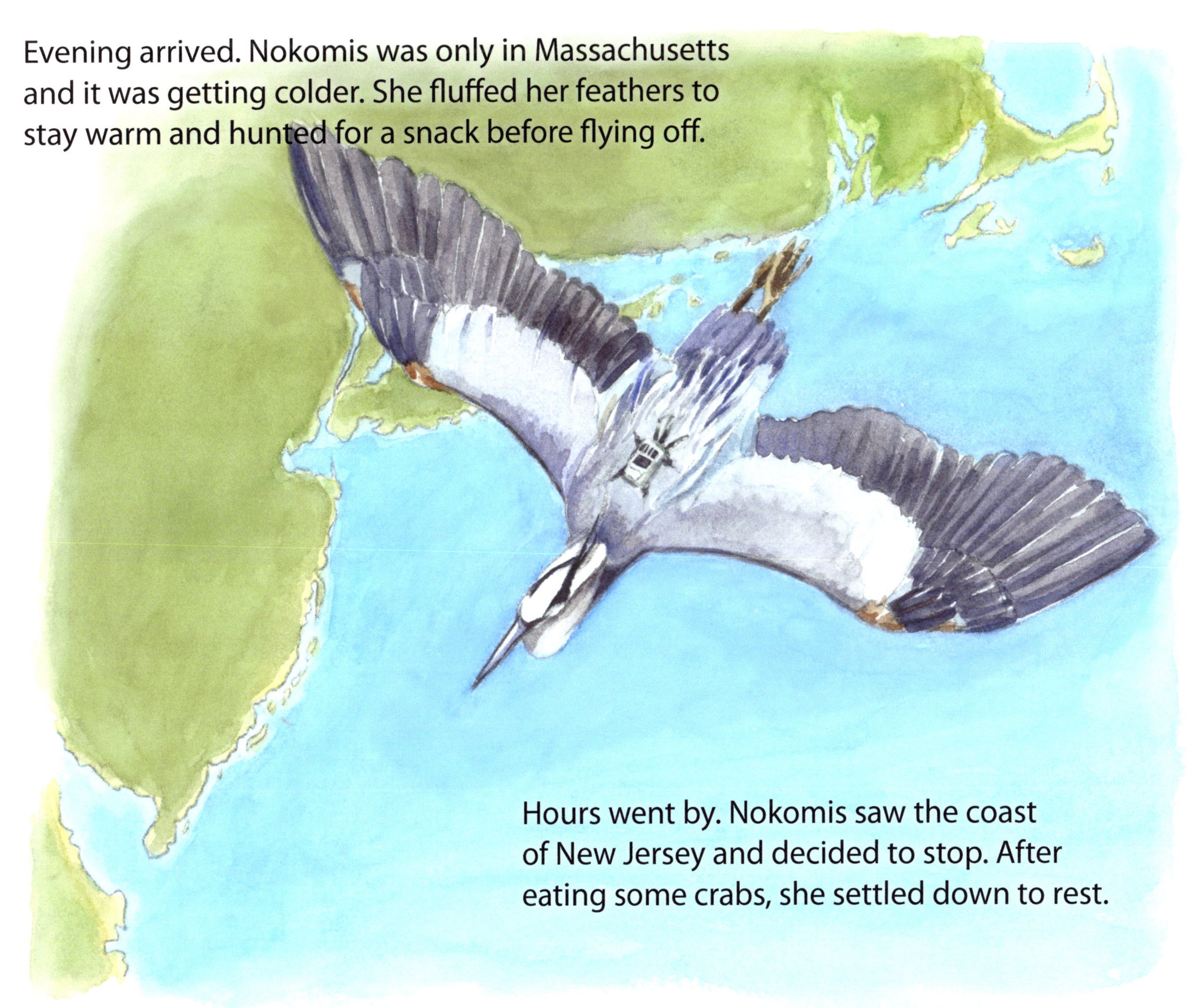

Evening arrived. Nokomis was only in Massachusetts and it was getting colder. She fluffed her feathers to stay warm and hunted for a snack before flying off.

Hours went by. Nokomis saw the coast of New Jersey and decided to stop. After eating some crabs, she settled down to rest.

When Nokomis woke, she saw dark clouds in the sky. She flapped her wings to take off but was blown backwards by a strong wind! Nokomis tried again, using her long legs to push off the ground while flapping her strong wings.

It was no use. Nokomis knew it was not safe to fly in a storm.
She found shelter and stayed in place for two more days.

After the storm passed, Nokomis flew for 30 hours straight over the open ocean! She ate and rested in the Bahamas and Cuba before finally reaching her wintering grounds in Haiti. There she found a safe place to stay near a rice field outside a small village where there was plenty of water, food, and warm weather.

In mid-March, it was time for Nokomis to make the long journey home to Maine. She would need to stop to rest and eat many times on the way. She flew toward one of her favorite resting areas only to find a building where a pond used to be! Nokomis was tired and hungry but had no choice but to keep flying.

An hour later Nokomis saw a new pond that looked promising. As she landed, she noticed two other great blue herons wading in the water. They were also on their way back to New England. The three of them ate before taking much needed naps.

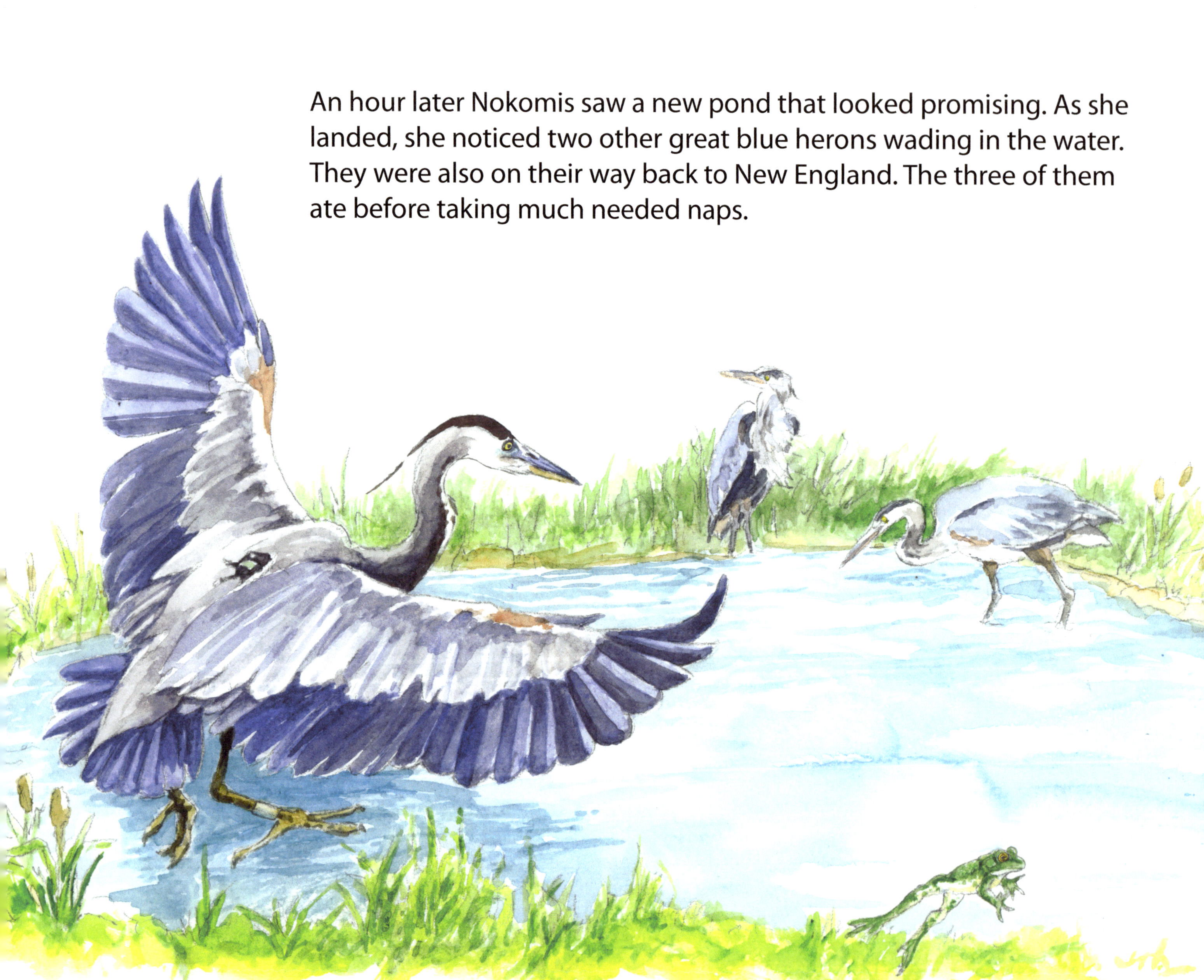

After traveling for about three weeks, Nokomis arrived in Maine. And guess where she decided to stay? Near Nokomis Regional High School! Nokomis flew to her old nesting colony. She was finally home.

Her mate was waiting for her when she arrived. He began
to bring sticks for her to build a nest in a pine tree. The nest
was so high in the tree that they could see Sebasticook Lake
in the distance. But Nokomis and her mate weren't the only
ones who were happy to be home. Nokomis High School
students were glad to see the great blue herons return. The
students watched over and studied the heron colony to learn
more about the herons and the herons' habitat. This included
marking and measuring trees in the colony and using sound
recorders to listen for any kind of disturbances at the nests.

Nokomis laid three eggs. She and her mate took turns sitting on the eggs for 30 days. The three baby birds were small, fuzzy, and very hungry when they hatched!

Nokomis and her mate also took turns hunting for food. They looked for salamanders, turtles, snakes, fish, and any other food items they could find.

Two and a half months later, the nestlings were almost as big as their parents and able to fly. Soon after, they left the nest to start their own journey.

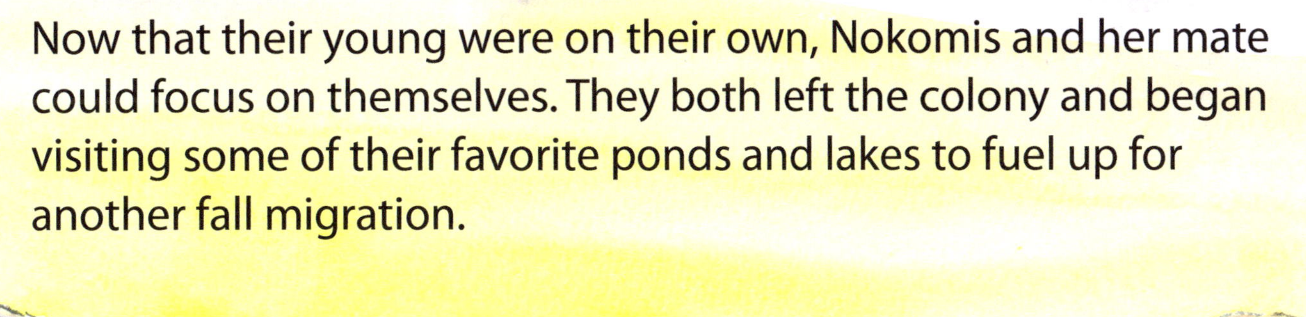

Now that their young were on their own, Nokomis and her mate could focus on themselves. They both left the colony and began visiting some of their favorite ponds and lakes to fuel up for another fall migration.

GREAT BLUE HERON FUN FACTS

✓ Nokomis was tracked by biologists for 4 years and 7 months. During that time, she traveled approximately 30,000 miles! That means she could have circled the Earth at least once!

✓ A Great Blue Heron's wingspan can be over 6 feet wide. Hold your arms straight out from your sides: How wide is your "wingspan"?

✓ Great Blue Herons are the largest of the North American herons.

✓ There is an all white heron found in southern Florida. It is called the Great White Heron.

✓ When migrating, Great Blue Herons have been recorded flying as high as 4,000 feet (1,219 meters) above sea level and as fast as 60 miles per hour (97 kilometers per hour).

QUESTIONS TO THINK ABOUT

✓   Can you name 3 food items that Nokomis ate on her journey?

✓   Can you identify 3 habitats where Nokomis stopped on her trip?
     Hint: a habitat is a place where an animal lives.

✓   Water pollution and climate change affect Great Blue Heron food and habitat. Can you think of
     other items that might affect Great Blue Herons?

✓   Do you still have questions about Nokomis in particular, or Great Blue Herons in general? Visit
     Maine's Great Blue Heron website here: https://www.maine.gov/wordpress/ifwheron/

✓   What sounds does a Great Blue Heron make? Cornell's Lab of Ornithology is a helpful resource:
     https://www.allaboutbirds.org/news/

9 798987 347119